D0713477

A Kid's Guide to Drawing America™

How to Draw Washington's Sights and Symbols

Aileen Weintraub

The Rosen Publishing Group's
PowerKids Press™
New York

Published in 2002 by The Rosen Publishing Group, Inc.
29 East 21st Street, New York, NY 10010

First Edition

Editor: Joanne Riethoff
Book Design: Kim Sonsky
Layout Design: Colin Dizengoff

Illustration Credits: Jamie Grecco
Photo Credits: p. 7 © Philip James Corwin/CORBIS; pp. 8–9 © University of Puget Sound, Permanent Collection; p. 12, 14 © One Mile Up, Incorporated; pp. 16, 28 © Michael T. Sedam/CORBIS; p 18 © Wolfgang Kaehler/CORBIS; p. 20 © Darrell Gulin/CORBIS; p. 22 © Paul A. Souders/CORBIS; p. 24 © Roger Ressmeyer/CORBIS; p. 26 © Douglas Peebles/CORBIS.

Weintraub, Aileen
    How to draw Washington's sights and symbols / Aileen Weintraub.
        p. cm. — (A kid's guide to drawing America)
    Includes index.
    Summary: This book explains how to draw some of Washington's sights and symbols, including the state seal, the official flower, and the Space Needle.
    ISBN 0-8239-6104-4
    1. Emblems, State—Washington (State)—Juvenile literature 2. Washington (State)—In art—Juvenile literature 3. Drawing—Technique—Juvenile literature
[1. Emblems, State—Washington (State)   2. Washington (State) 3. Drawing—Technique] I. Title II. Series
    743'.8'99797—dc21

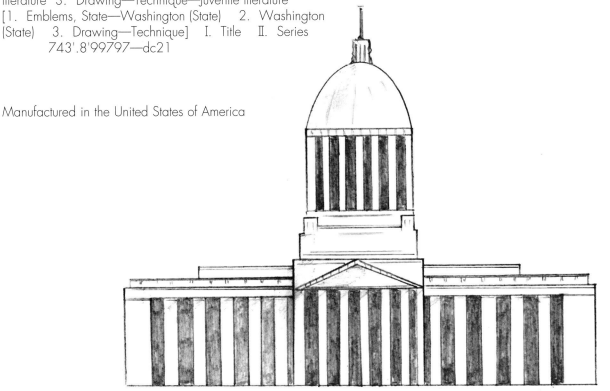

Manufactured in the United States of America

CONTENTS

Let's Draw Washington

Before Washington became a state, it was part of what was known as Oregon country. Spanish, British, and American explorers all visited this area. Meriwether Lewis and William Clark were two explorers whom the United States sent to explore the Northwest. In 1805, they reached the area where Washington is now. Their trip helped the United States claim Washington. In 1853, Congress created the Washington Territory from the northern part of Oregon country. On November 11, 1889, Washington became the forty-second state. Washington is named for George Washington, the first president of the United States. This is the only state that is named for a president.

Washington has more than 1,000 dams. The Grand Coulee dam, built on the Columbia River, is the biggest concrete dam in the world. It is 5,223 feet (1,592 m) long and is 550 feet (168 m) tall. It provides much of the Northwest with electrical power.

Washington is also home to Mount Rainier, the highest mountain in the Pacific Northwest. Mount Rainier is really an active volcano. Its last eruption was about 150 years ago. It is 14,410 feet (4,392 m) high.

This book will teach you about some of the sights and symbols of Washington. Each drawing begins with an easy shape. From there you will add more shapes until your drawing is complete. Each new step is shown in red. To add shading, tilt your pencil to the side and rub back and forth. The most important thing is to have fun!

You will need the following supplies to draw Washington's sights and symbols:

- A sketch pad
- An eraser
- A number 2 pencil
- A pencil sharpener

These are some of the shapes and drawing terms you need to know to draw Washington's sights and symbols:

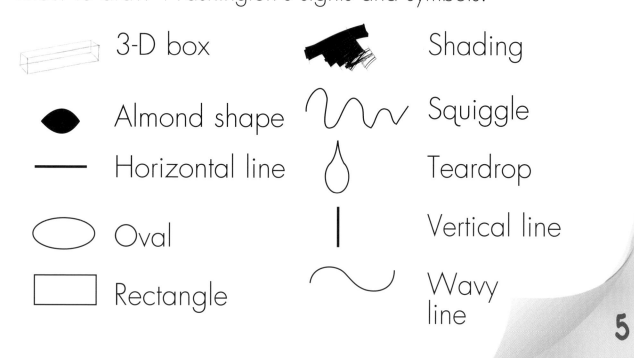

3-D box

Shading

Almond shape

Squiggle

Horizontal line

Teardrop

Oval

Vertical line

Rectangle

Wavy line

The Evergreen State

Washington's nickname is the Evergreen State. C. T. Conover was the person who came up with Washington's nickname. He chose the name because of all the forests in Washington. Much of the western part of the state is a temperate rain forest. This means there is a lot of rain in Washington. When most people think of a rain forest, they think of the hot, humid temperatures of the Amazon rain forest in South America. A temperate rain forest has cooler temperatures, but just as much rain. A rain forest can average 136 inches (354 cm) of rain in a year! This makes Washington a very green state.

The Hoh Rain Forest is in Olympic National Park. This park is also home to Mount Olympus. Blue Glacier is one of six glaciers that flow down Mount Olympus. Another important park in Washington is Peace Arch State Park. This park features a giant concrete arch. Half of this arch is in Washington and the other half is in Canada. The arch represents the friendship between Canada and the United States.

All the rain that falls in Washington helps to create forests of evergreen trees, like this one in the Olympic Peninsula, Washington.

Artist in Washington

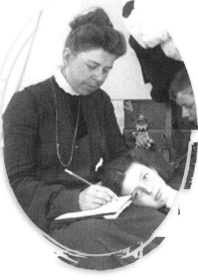

Abby Rhoda Williams Hill was born in 1861, in Grinnell, Iowa. She moved to Washington in 1889. Hill was a landscape artist who loved to paint the mountain scenery of the Northwest. She spent much of her life painting in the wilderness. She painted the Cascade Mountain Range, waterfalls, snow, trees, and other nature

Abby Rhoda Williams Hill

scenes. She was also known as the railway artist, because she had contracts with major railway companies. Railways wanted artists to publicize the beauty of the Northwest through their artwork. This way tourists would see the art and want to ride the trains to different parts of the country. Hill's work has been exhibited

Hill wrote and decorated this letter. It is done with pencil on paper and was written on December 25, 1895.

8

at the St. Louis World's Fair, the Lewis and Clark Exposition, and the Alaska-Yukon Exposition. Hill died in 1943. She left behind more than 100 canvases. Some of her work shows bright colors with broad brush strokes. Hill will forever be known as the artist who spent most of her time outdoors so she could be close to nature.

This painting, entitled *Looking Down Lake Chelan*, was painted in 1903. It measures 42" x 29" (107 cm x 74 cm). The colors and the broad brush strokes create a dreamy atmosphere with this landscape.

Map of Washington

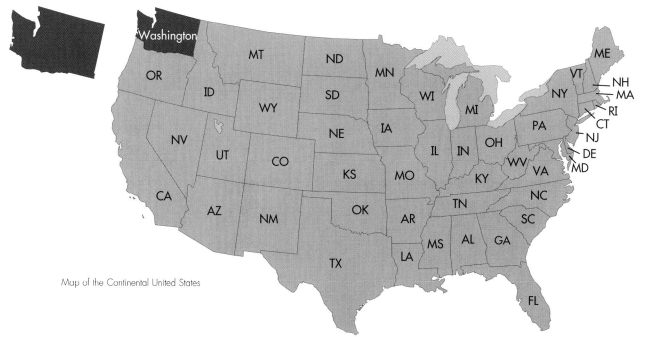

Map of the Continental United States

Washington is in the northwestern United States. The Pacific Ocean lies to its west. Oregon is to the south and Idaho is to the east. The country of Canada is to the north. Washington covers 70,637 square miles (182,949 sq km). It has about 3,000 miles (4,828 km) of shoreline. The Columbia River flows along the southern border and into the northeastern part of Washington from Canada. The Grand Coulee dam creates a reservoir known as Lake Roosevelt. It is 130 miles (209 km) long. This lake is now part of the Lake Roosevelt National Recreation Area. Many people enjoy all kinds of outdoor activities here, such as camping and hiking.

1

Start by drawing a rectangle.

2

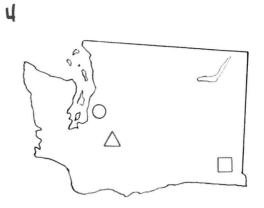

Draw the shape of Washington using squiggles and wavy lines.

3

Erase extra lines, and draw a circle to mark Seattle. Now draw the shape of Lake Roosevelt.

4

Draw a square to mark Umatilla National Forest and a triangle for Mount Rainier National Park.

5

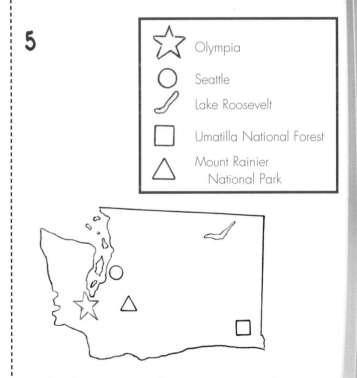

☆ Olympia

◯ Seattle

⌒ Lake Roosevelt

☐ Umatilla National Forest

△ Mount Rainier National Park

To finish your map, draw a star to mark Olympia, the capital of Washington. You can also make a key in the upper right corner to mark Washington's points of interest.

The State Seal

The Washington state seal was created in 1889. It has a very simple design. The center of the seal shows George Washington. The words around the seal read "The Seal of the State of Washington, 1889." The seal was created by a jeweler named Charles Talcott. Originally members of the state government had designed a seal based on the state's landscape. It was to include the port of Tacoma, Mount Rainier, and livestock. The state officials took the design to Talcott, so he could make an engraving of it. Talcott didn't like the design. He sketched out a design using a postage stamp of George Washington for reference. The government officials were pleased with the new design. Although the seal was created in 1889, it wasn't made official until 1967.

1

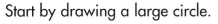

Start by drawing a large circle.

2

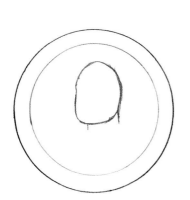

Add a smaller circle inside the large one. Draw a rough oval for the shape of George Washington's head and two small lines for his neck.

3

Redraw the shape of Washington's head to show the chin and jaw. Add a coat using straight and slanted lines. Erase extra lines.

4

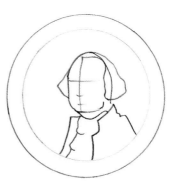

Draw in his hair, and add a cross shape over his face to help place the eyes, the nose, and the mouth. Draw the ruffles in the coat.

5

Draw in Washington's face. Use curved lines for the eyebrows, the lips, and the nose. Use ovals for his eyes. Then erase the extra lines.

6

Add the words "THE SEAL OF THE STATE OF WASHINGTON" around the edge of the seal and the date 1889. Then add shading and detail, and you're done.

The State Flag

This flag has a dark green background with the state seal in the center. The Washington flag is the only state flag that is green. It is also the only flag to have a picture of George Washington on it. Washington's face is placed on a blue background, and the surrounding border is either gold or yellow depending on the flag. Sometimes the flag has a gold or yellow fringe on it. Even though the state is named for George Washington, Washington himself never traveled that far west. The flag was officially adopted in 1923. Before this flag was used, many citizens in Washington flew a similar flag. It had George Washington's profile on it, and the colors were blue and gold.

1

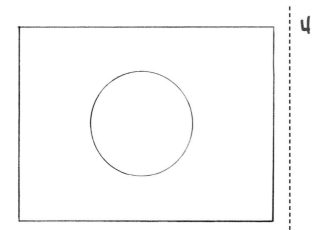

Start by drawing a large rectangle for the flag's field and a circle in the center.

2

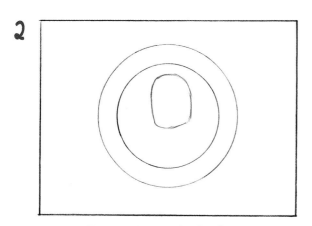

Add a smaller circle inside the large one, and draw a rough oval for the shape of Washington's head.

3

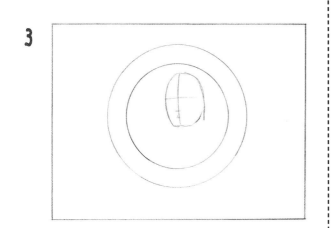

Add a cross shape over his face to help place the eyes, the nose, and the mouth.

4

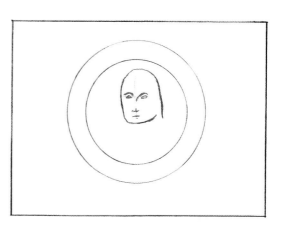

Draw in Washington's eyes, nose, and mouth. Erase extra lines.

5

Draw in Washington's hair and coat.

6

Add the words "THE SEAL OF THE STATE OF WASHINGTON" around the edge of the seal and the date 1889. Then add shading and detail, and you're done.

15

The Pink Rhododendron

In 1892, the women of Washington state held a women-only election to vote on Washington's state flower. Women in Washington wanted an official flower to enter in the floral exhibit of the 1893 World's Fair in Chicago. There were many suggestions for what the flower should be. A woman named Alsora Hayner Fry nominated the coast rhododendron. Fifteen thousand women voted on the state flower. Fifty-three percent voted for the coast rhododendron, and it became the state flower on February 10, 1893. It wasn't until February 10, 1949, that the state made it official. In 1959, the law was changed to specify the pink rhododendron.

1

Start by drawing a circle for the center of the flower.

2

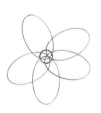

Now add five ovals around the center for petals.

3

Using the ovals as guides, draw in the shape of the petals.

4

Erase extra lines.

5

Repeat steps one through four until you've made a large, circular blossom of flowers. You can also add triangular leaves here if you like.

6

Add shading and detail to your flower, and you're done.

The Western Hemlock

In 1946, a newspaper from Oregon ran an article that pointed out Washington did not have a state tree. That newspaper's staff picked out the western hemlock for their neighbor state. A Washington newspaper staff decided to pick their own tree, the red cedar. However, a Washington state representative named George Adams agreed that the western hemlock would be a better choice. These trees are very important for timber, which is important to Washington's economy. He asked the state government to make the western hemlock Washington's tree. The state government adopted the western hemlock as its state tree in 1947. Western hemlocks can grow to be 200 feet (61 m) tall.

1

Start by drawing a long, thin triangle for the tree trunk.

2

Add branches to help you place the leaf clusters.

3

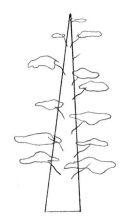

Draw rough oval shapes for the shape of the leaf clusters.

4

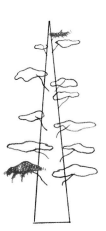

Use the ovals as a guide. Draw in the needles by using short, straight lines.

5

Continue drawing the needles. Erase extra lines. Add curvy lines in the tree trunk.

6

Shade in the tree trunk. Add more clusters of leaves if you like, and the tree is complete.

The Willow Goldfinch

In 1928, schoolchildren from the state of Washington were asked to select a state bird. They chose the meadowlark. Seven other states already had the meadowlark as their state bird. In 1931, the Washington Federation of Women's Clubs decided to vote for another state bird. This time the willow goldfinch won. At this point, Washington had two state birds, so the government asked the schoolchildren to vote again. In 1951, children voted for the goldfinch. The willow goldfinch is a yellow bird with black on its tail, wings, and head. It is a small bird reaching about 4 ½ inches (11 cm) in length. The willow goldfinch is also known as a cheerful singer and a graceful flier.

1

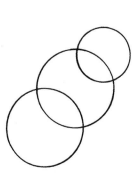

Start by drawing three circles for the rough shape of the bird.

2

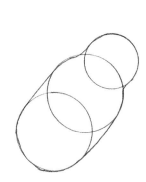

Connect your circles to form the shape of the bird's body.

3

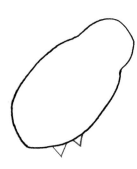

Erase extra lines, and add two triangles for the tops of the legs.

4

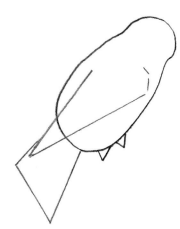

Add two triangle shapes, one for the wing and one for the tail.

5

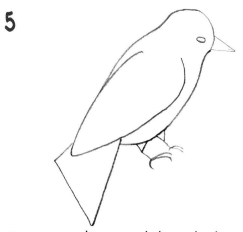

Erase extra lines, and draw the legs and the feet. Add a triangle for the beak and an oval for the eye.

6

Add shading and detail to your bird, and you're done. You can also add a branch if you like.

The Bald Eagle

When settlers first arrived in what is now the state of Washington, it is thought that the bald eagle population was close to 6,500. By 1980, there were only 210 known bald eagles in the state. The use of pesticides, the cutting down of forests, and the fishing industry all contributed to its decline. Fortunately the bald eagle population is growing. In 1998, there were 664 eagle nests in Washington. It is thought that there are now more than 4,000 bald eagles in Washington.

Bald eagles are from 36 to 43 inches (91–109 cm) long and have a wingspan of about 8 feet (2.5 m). They have brown bodies, white heads and tails, and yellow beaks, eyes, and feet.

1

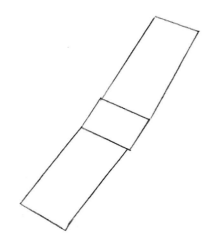

Start by drawing three rectangles for the rough shape of the bird.

2

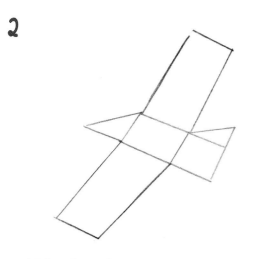

Add five lines for the tail as shown and a triangle shape for the head.

3

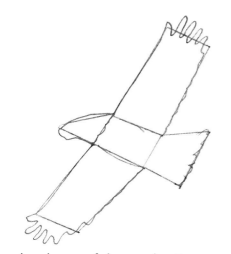

Draw the shape of the eagle. Erase any extra lines.

4

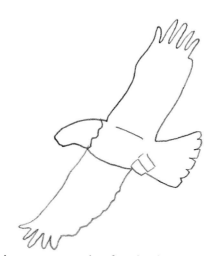

Add two rectangles for the legs. Notice that they are slightly curved.

5

Add feet, a triangle-shaped beak, and an eye.

6

Add shading and detail to your bird, and you're done. You can smudge your shading for added effect.

23

Mount Saint Helens

Mount Saint Helens is a volcano that is part of the Cascade Mountain Range in Washington. This volcano erupted on May 18, 1980, at 8:32 A.M. Gray ash from the explosion covered the sky in the eastern part of Washington. The eruption lasted for 9 hours. The north side of the volcano collapsed in an avalanche. This eruption killed 65 people and destroyed almost 230 square miles (596 sq km) of forest, including wildlife. Eruptions continued until 1986, building layers of lava. The dome of earth that the lava created is 920 feet (280 m) high.

In 1982, the U.S. government created the National Volcanic Monument for research and education at Mount Saint Helens.

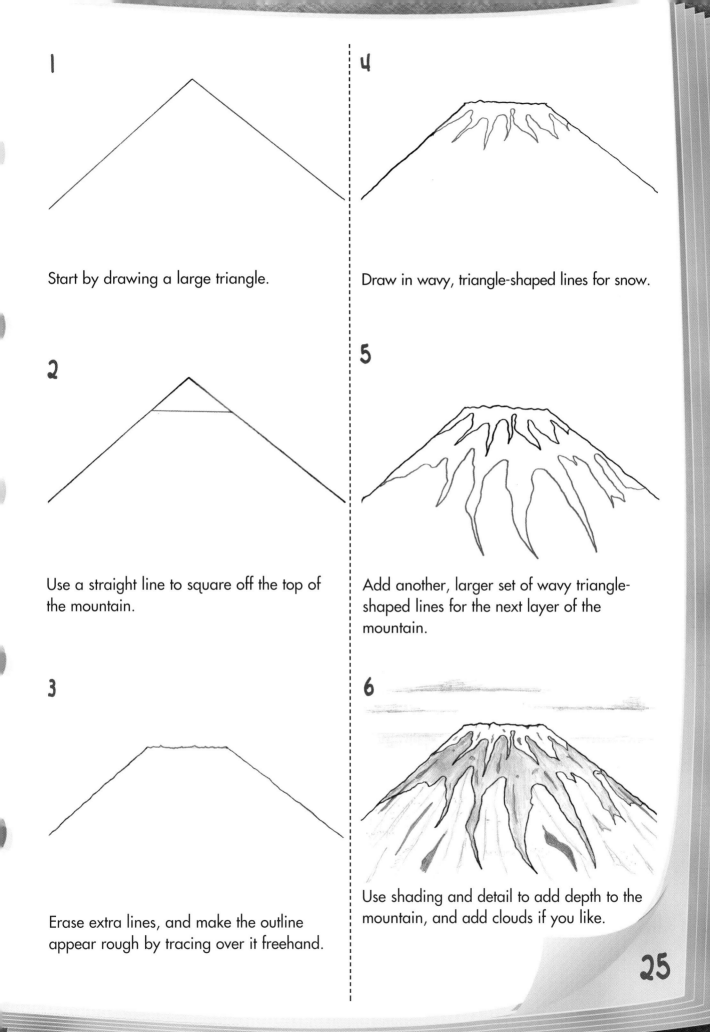

1

Start by drawing a large triangle.

2

Use a straight line to square off the top of the mountain.

3

Erase extra lines, and make the outline appear rough by tracing over it freehand.

4

Draw in wavy, triangle-shaped lines for snow.

5

Add another, larger set of wavy triangle-shaped lines for the next layer of the mountain.

6

Use shading and detail to add depth to the mountain, and add clouds if you like.

The Space Needle

The Space Needle was built in Seattle for the 1962 World's Fair. In 1959, a designer named Edward E. Carlson thought of the idea for the Space Needle. The needle stands 605 feet (184 m) tall. It is made of steel. The underground foundation is 30 feet (9 m) deep and 120 feet (36.5 m) across. This foundation is made of cement. At the top of the needle there is an observation deck and a revolving restaurant. The needle is built to withstand harsh winds and even earthquakes. The colors of paint used on the Space Needle are called astronaut white, orbital olive, reentry red, and galaxy gold. The needle was finally completed in December 1961. It opened on April 21, 1962, the first day of the World's Fair.

1

Start by drawing two triangular shapes.

2

Add two more triangles for the supports.

3

Add two rectangles to start the top.

4

Add two slanted rectangles above the first two to form a disc shape. Add another rectangle on top of those.

5

Draw the top using a triangle and a square. Add the peak using a thin line.

6

Erase extra lines. Add shading and detail, like small windows and clouds, and your Space Needle is done.

Washington's Capitol

The current capitol building is really Washington's third capitol. Ernest Flagg designed the current capitol in 1893, after Washington became a state. Two architects named Walter Wilder and Harry White from New York were chosen to carry out Flagg's original design more than 15 years later. Work began on the foundation of the building in 1919. Construction of the building started in 1922 and was finished in 1928. The building rises to 287 feet (87 m) at the dome, which is the largest in the world. The landscape around the capitol was designed by Olmstead Brothers–Landscape Architects. This company also designed Central Park in New York City.

1

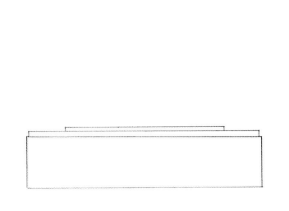

Draw three rectangles. The bottom one is much bigger than the others. Each rectangle is shorter than the one below it.

2

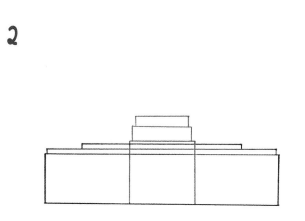

Add three more rectangles for the center of the building and the base of the dome.

3

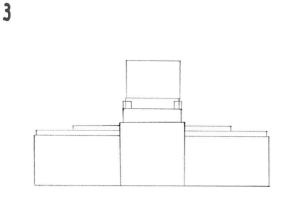

Erase extra lines and add two small squares and a large rectangle.

4

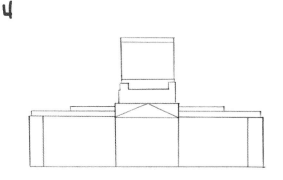

Add a rectangle on the top, two lines at the sides, and a triangle in the middle.

5

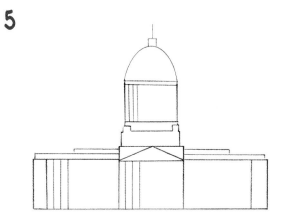

Draw a half oval, a rectangle, and a short, thin line to finish the dome. You can use thin rectangles to start drawing the columns.

6

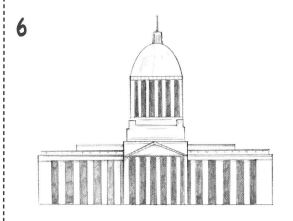

Finish the columns. Add shading and detail to your building, and you're done. You can also smudge your lines to make the shading more effective.

29

Washington State Facts

Statehood	November 11, 1889, 42nd state
Area	70,637 square miles (182,949 sq km)
Population	5,756,400
Capital	Olympia, population, 39,000
Most Populated City	Seattle, population, 524,700
Industries	Aerospace, tourism, food processing, forest products, paper products, industrial machinery, printing and publishing
Agriculture	Seafood, apples, dairy products, wheat, cattle, potatoes, hay
Flower	Pink rhododendron
Bird	Willow goldfinch
Motto	*Al-Ki*, "By And By"
Nickname	The Evergreen State
Song	"Washington, my home"
State Fruit	Apple
State Ship	*President Washington*
State Gem	Petrified wood
State Fish	Steelhead trout
State Dance	Square dance
State Folk Song	"Roll on, Columbia, Roll on"

Glossary

adopted (uh-DOPT-ed) To have accepted or approved something.

architects (AR-kih-tekts) People who design buildings.

avalanche (A-vuh-lanch) When a large amount of snow, ice, earth, or dirt slides down a mountainside.

decline (dih-KLYN) To drop in number.

engraving (en-GRAYV-ing) A design or picture that is cut into wood, stone, metal, or glass plates for printing.

eruption (ih-RUPT-shun) When a volcano has exploded.

exhibit (ig-ZIH-bit) Objects or pictures set aside for people to see.

exposition (ek-spuh-ZIH-shun) A public show.

foundation (fown-DAY-shun) The part on which other parts are built.

glaciers (GLAY-shurz) Large masses of ice that move down a mountain or along a valley.

landscape (LAND-skayp) A view of scenery on land.

lava (LAH-vuh) A hot liquid made of melted rock that comes out of a volcano.

legislature (LEH-jihs-lay-cher) A body of people that has the power to make or pass laws.

nominated (NAH-mih-nayt-ed) To have suggested someone or something for a particular position.

observation deck (ahb-sur-VAY-shun DEK) A place where one can look out at a view.

pesticides (PES-tih-sydz) Chemicals used to kill pests.

rain forest (RAYN FOR-est) A wet area with many kinds of plants and animals.

reservoir (REH-zuh-vwahr) A stored body of water.

temperate (TEM-pur-it) Moderate in respect to temperature.

territory (TEHR-uh-tor-ee) Land that is controlled by a person or a group.

Index

Web Sites

To learn more about the sights and symbols of the state of Washington, check out these Web sites:
www.50states.com/washingt.htm
www.leg.wa.gov/legis/symbols/symbols.htm